POPULAR SONGS
HAL LEONARD STUDENT PIANO LIBRARY

ELEMENTARY/LATE-ELEMENTARY PIANO SOLOS

You Raise Me Up

Contemporary Christian Songs for Piano Solo

Arranged by Deborah Brady

CONTENTS

Edited by J. Mark Baker

ISBN 0-634-09032-1

HAL•LEONARD® CORPORATION
7777 W. BLUEMOUND RD. P.O. BOX 13819 MILWAUKEE, WI 53213

All I Need

Words and Music by Bethany Dillon,
Ed Cash and Dave Barnes
Arranged by Deborah Brady

Upbeat Pop feel, in "two" (𝅗𝅥 = 104)

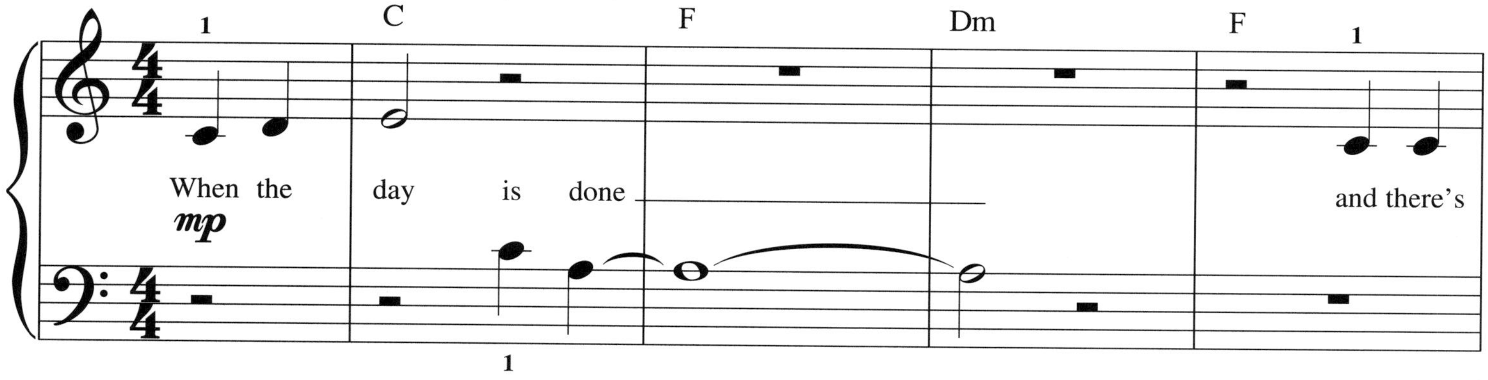

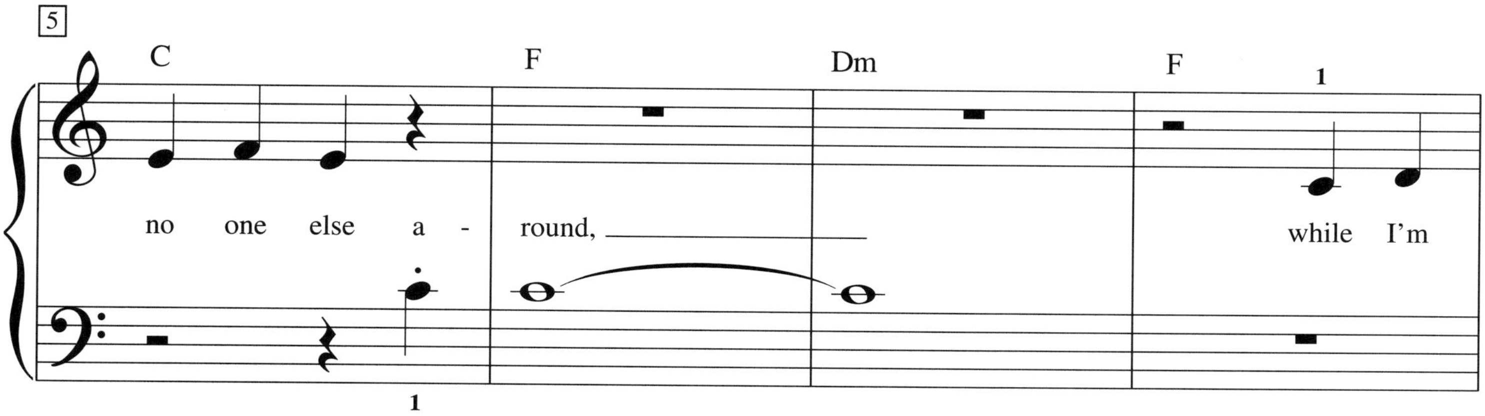

Accompaniment (Student plays one octave higher than written.)

Upbeat Pop feel, in "two" (𝅗𝅥 = 104)

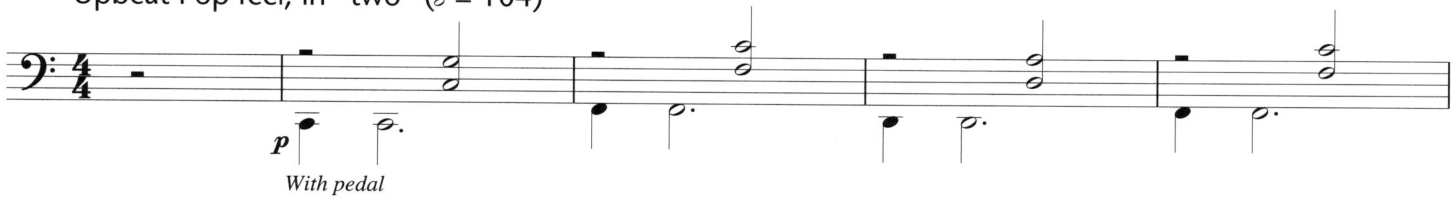

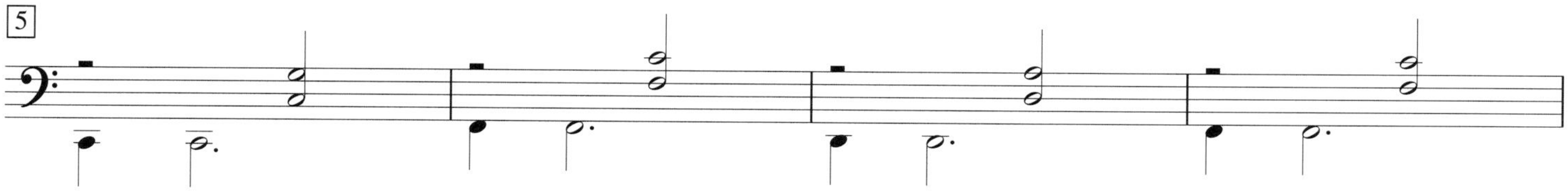

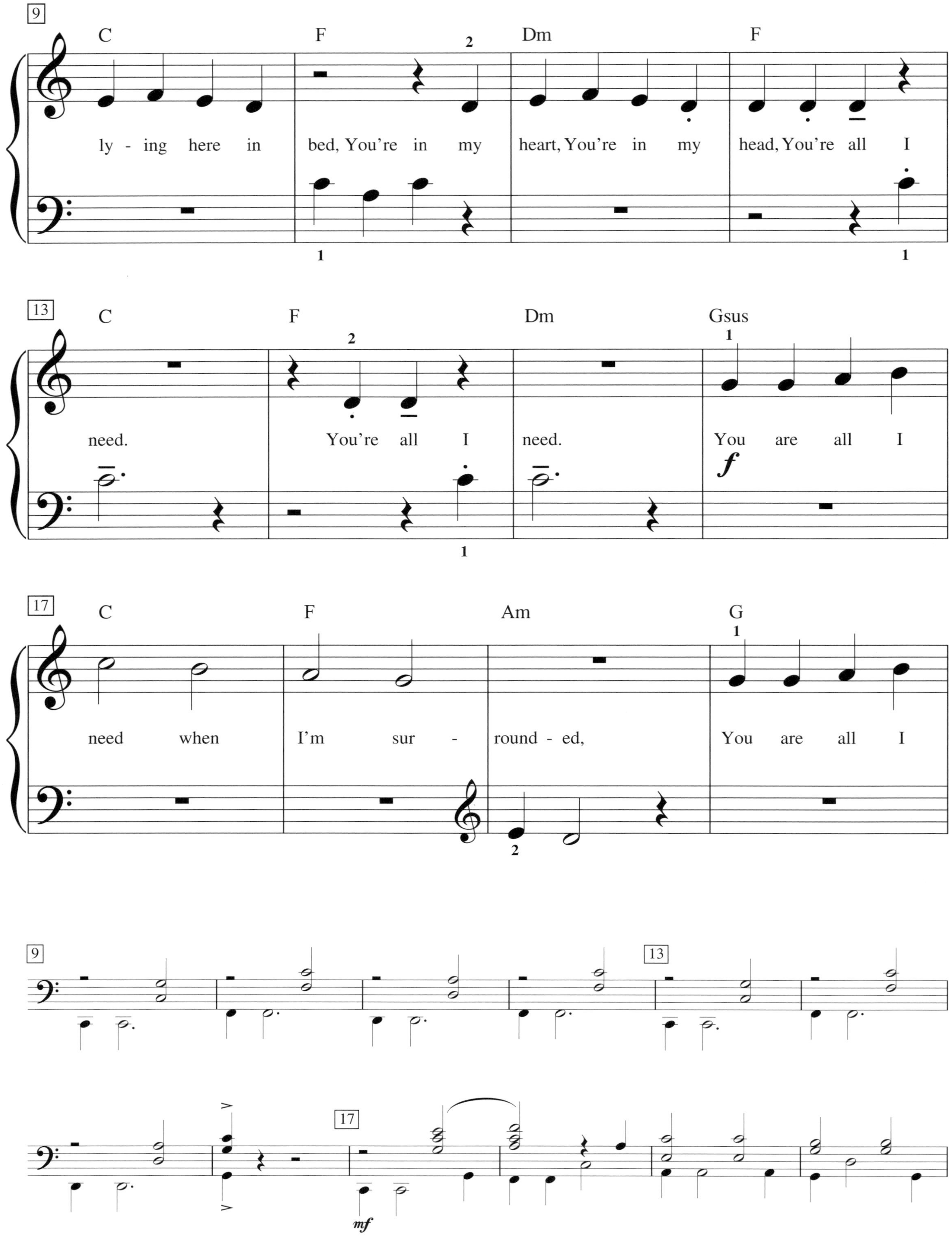
9
C F Dm F
ly - ing here in bed, You're in my heart, You're in my head, You're all I
13
C F Dm Gsus
need. You're all I need. You are all I
f
17
C F Am G
need when I'm sur - round - ed, You are all I
9
13
17
mf

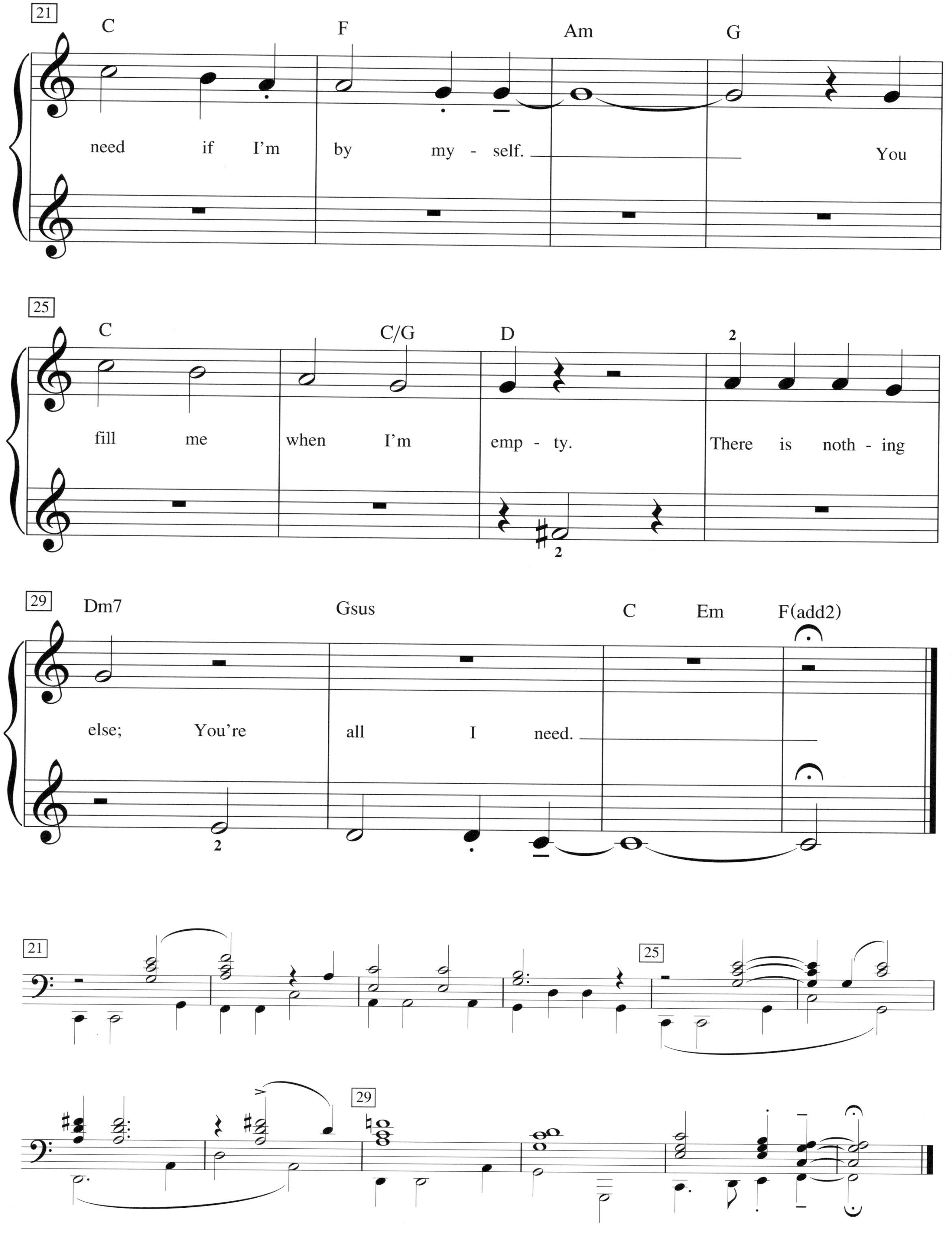
21
C
F
Am
G
need if I'm by my - self.
You
25
C
C/G
D
fill me when I'm emp - ty.
There is noth - ing
29
Dm7
Gsus
C
Em
F(add2)
else; You're all I need.
21
25
29

Forever

Words and Music by Chris Tomlin
Arranged by Deborah Brady

Strong Rock beat, in "two" (𝅗𝅥 = 120)

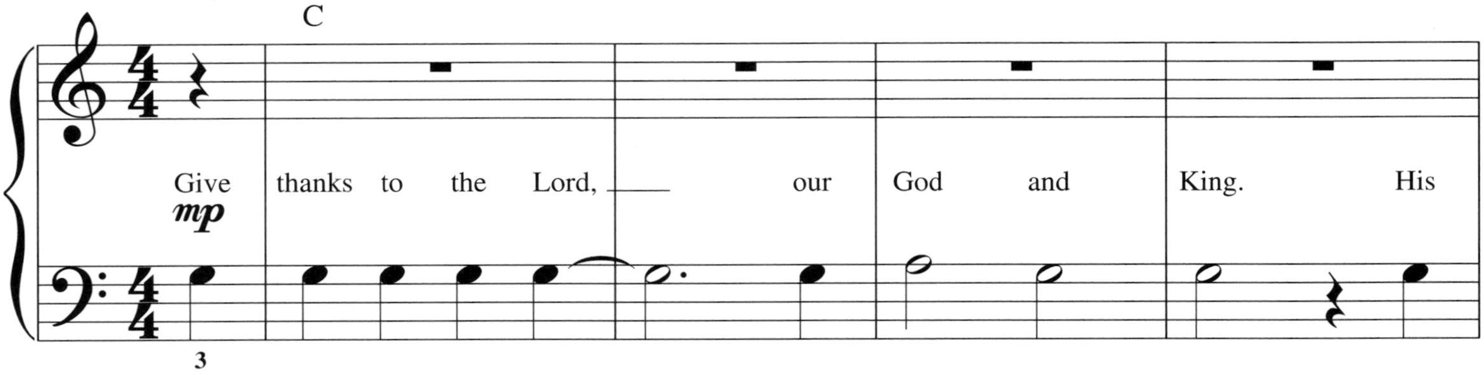

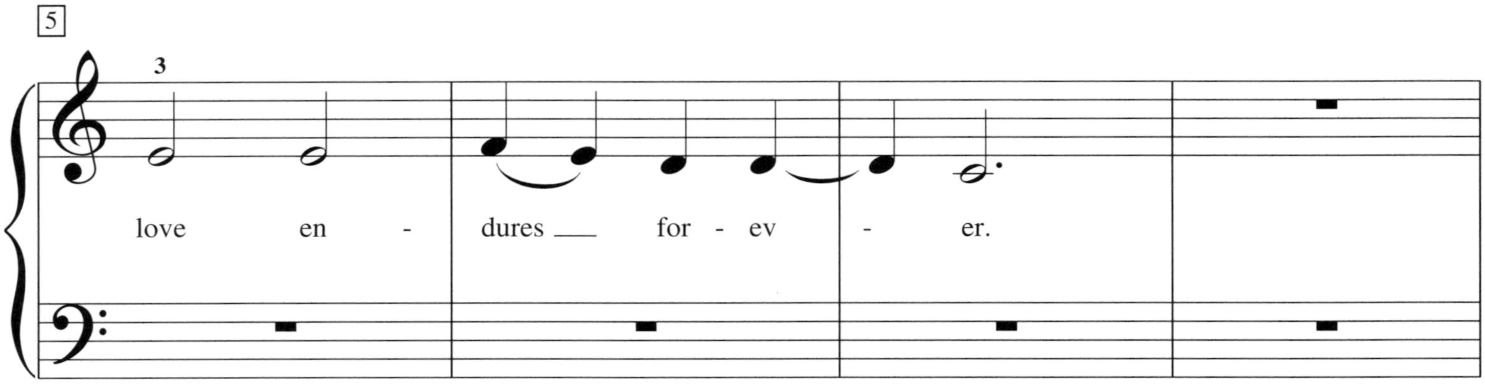

Accompaniment (Student plays one octave higher than written.)

Strong Rock beat, in "two" (𝅗𝅥 = 120)

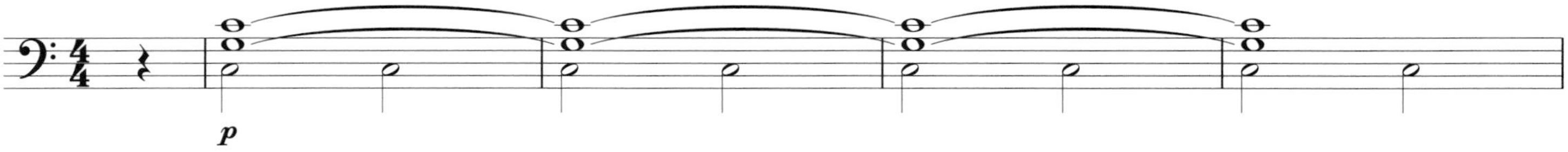

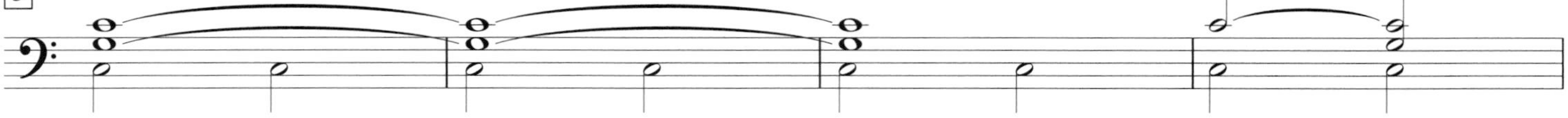

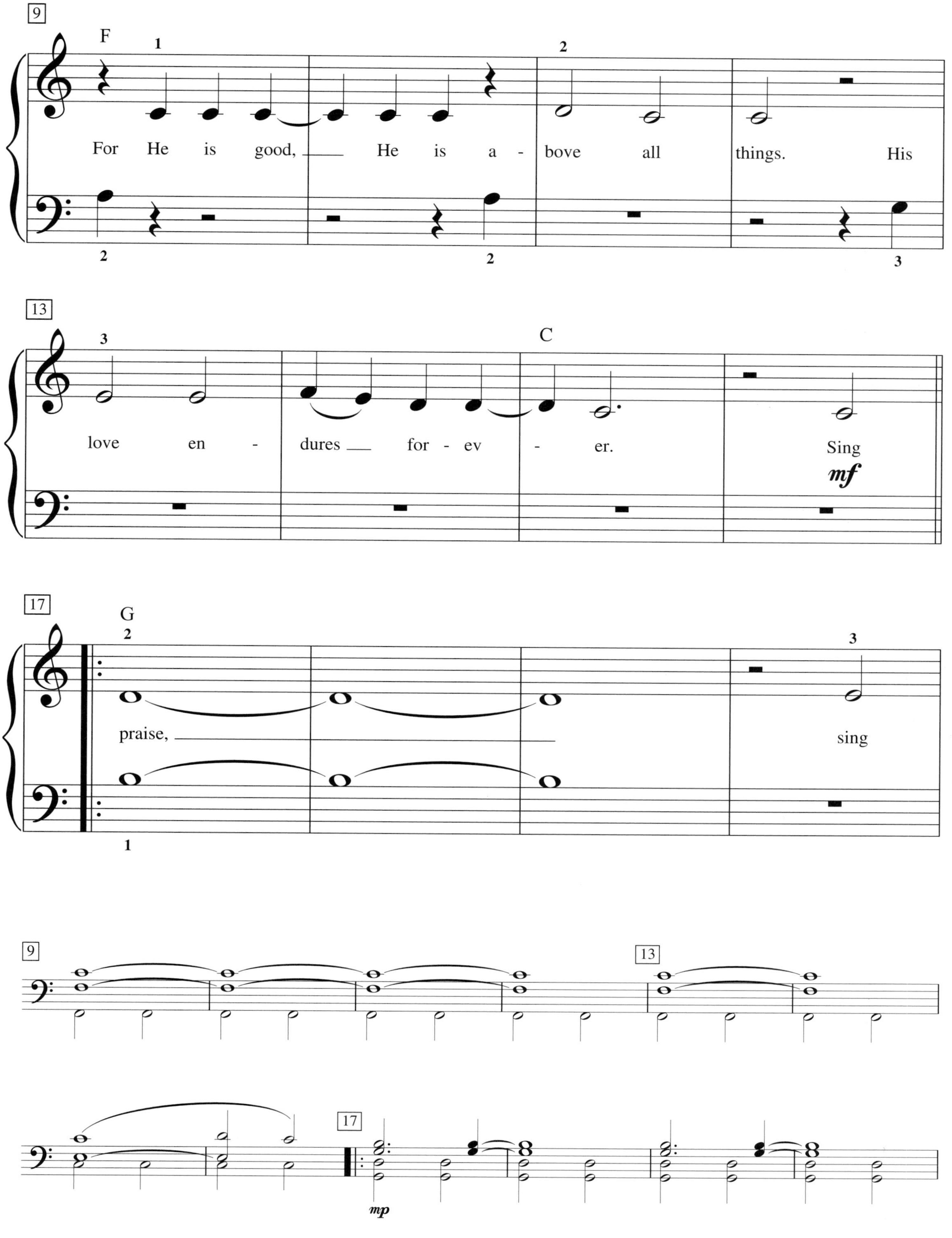

9
F
For He is good, He is a - bove all things. His
13
C
love en - dures for - ev - er.
Sing
mf
17
G
praise,
sing
9
13
17
mp

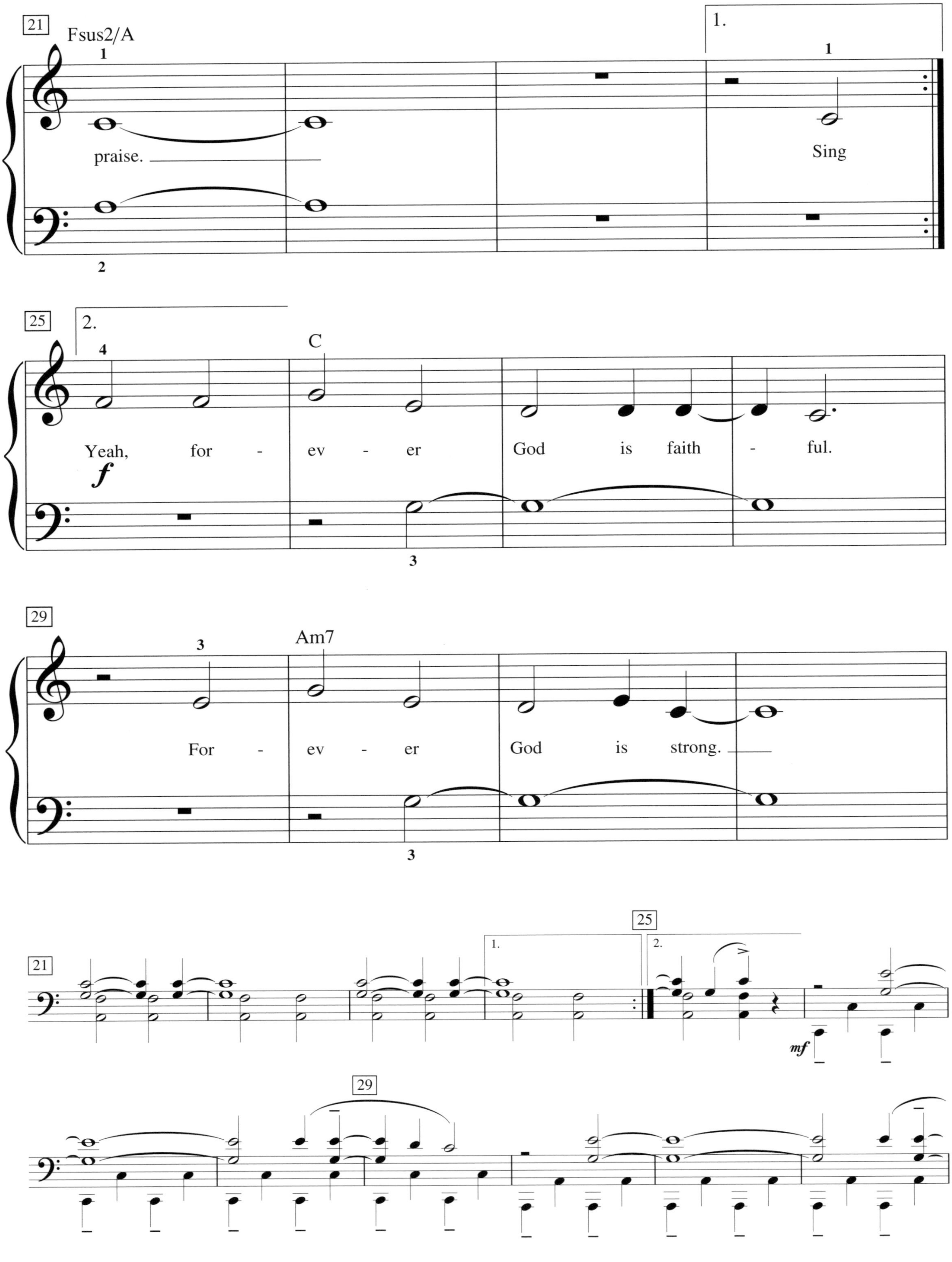
21
Fsus2/A
praise.
1.
Sing
25
2.
C
Yeah, for - ev - er God is faith - ful.
29
Am7
For - ev - er God is strong.
21
1.
25
2.
mf
29

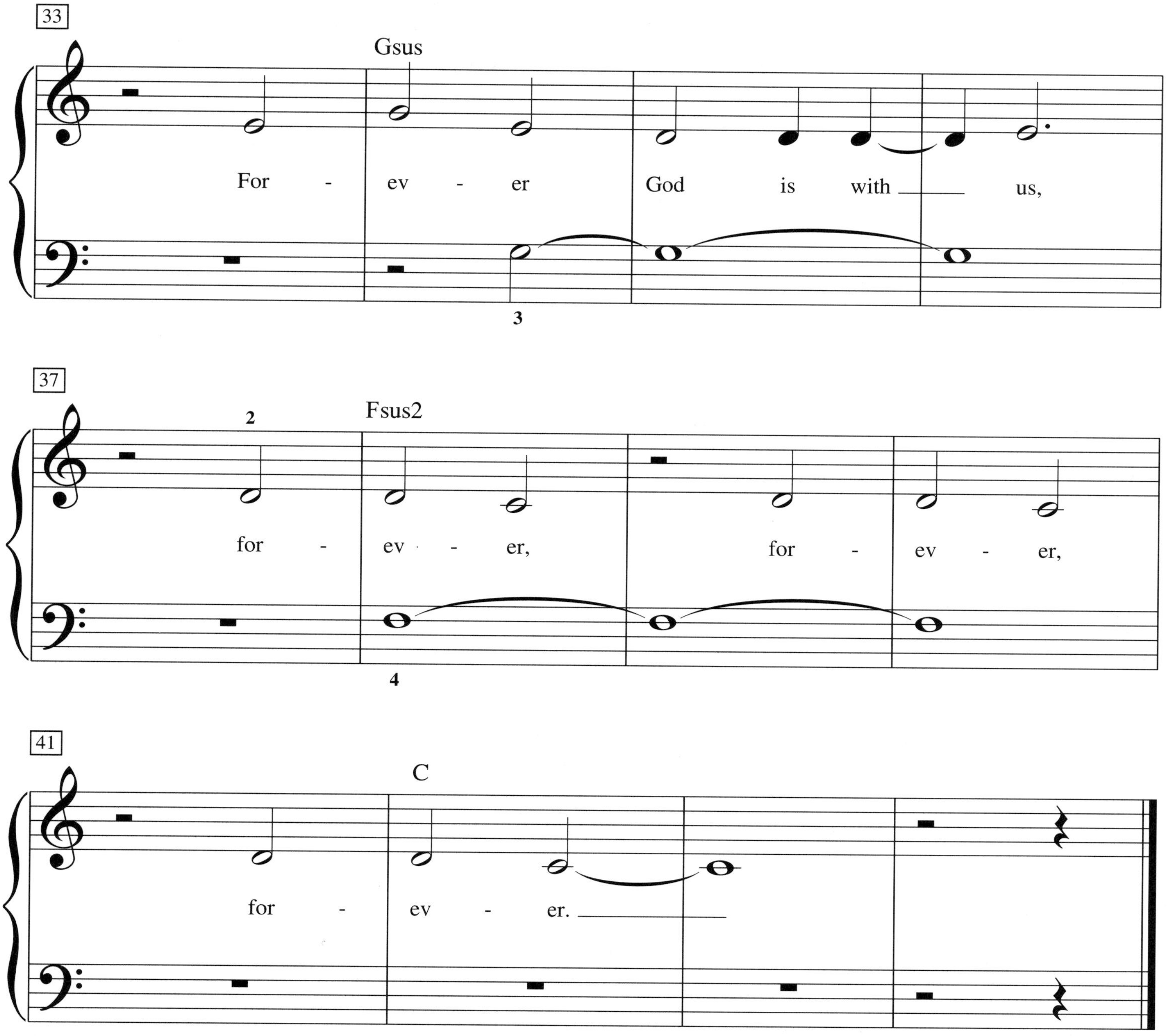
33
Gsus
For - ev - er God is with us,
3
37
2
Fsus2
for - ev - er, for - ev - er,
4
41
C
for - ev - er.

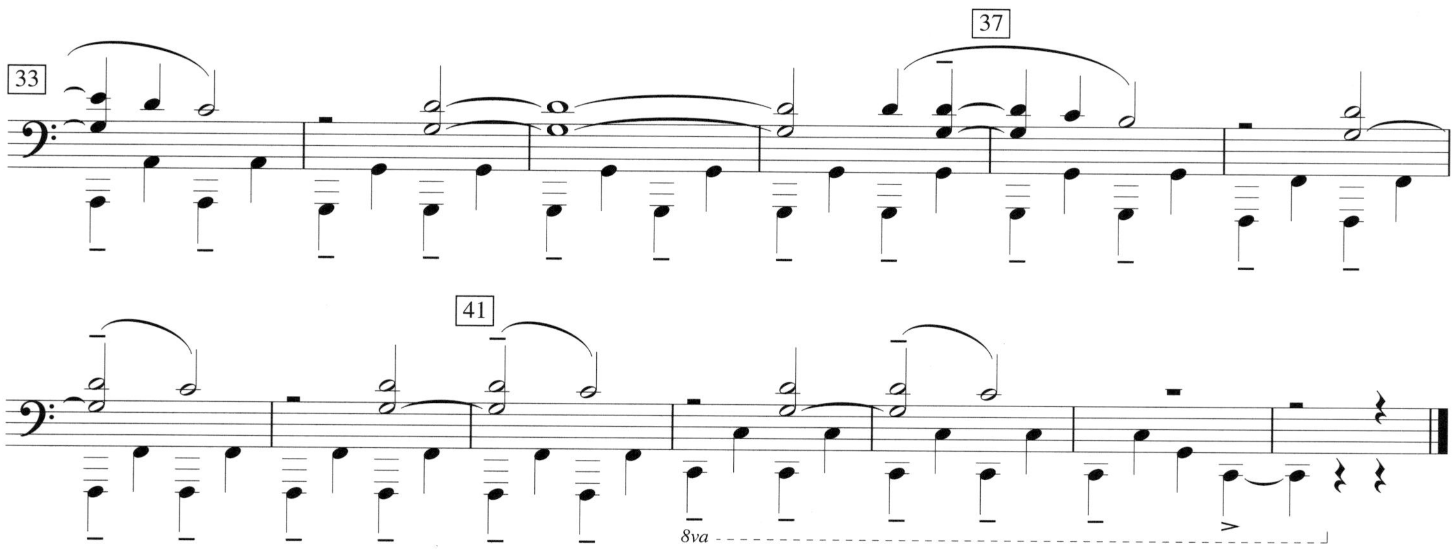
33
37
41
8va

Open The Eyes Of My Heart

Words and Music by Paul Baloche
Arranged by Deborah Brady

Meduim bright Pop, in "two" (𝅗𝅥 = 100)

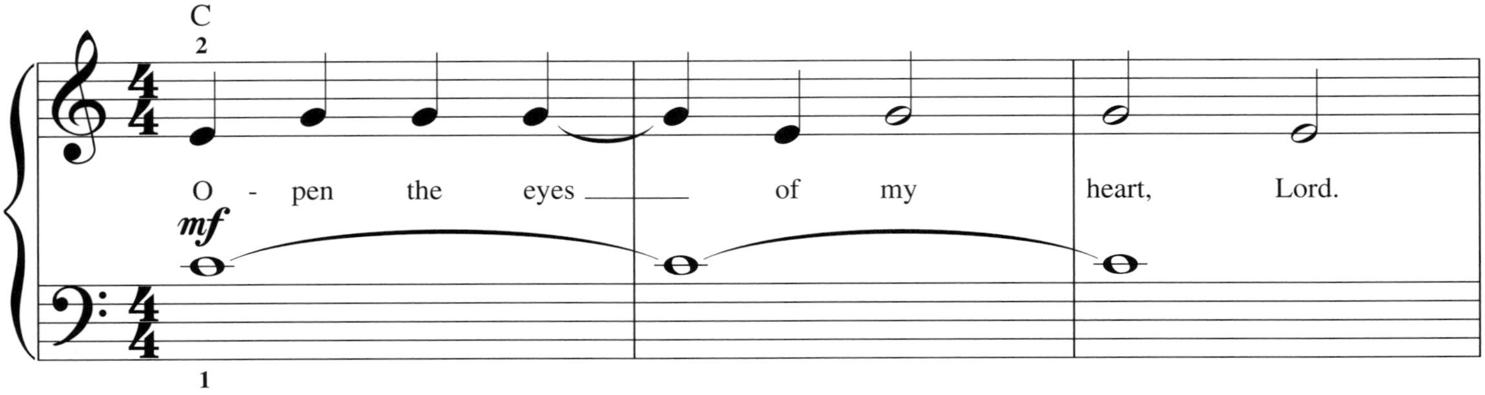

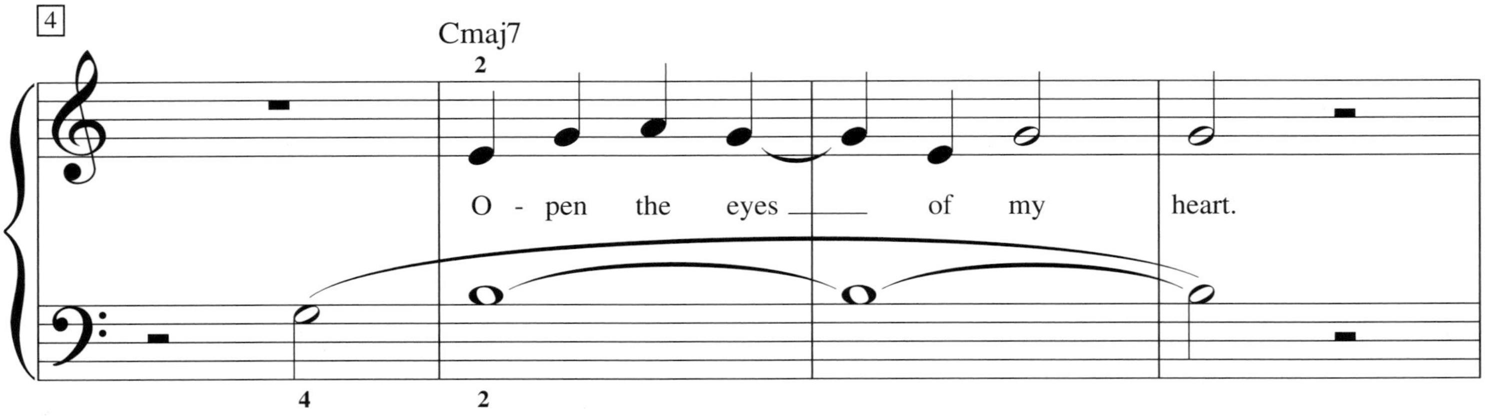

Accompaniment (Student plays one octave higher than written.)

Medium bright Pop, in "two" (𝅗𝅥 = 100)

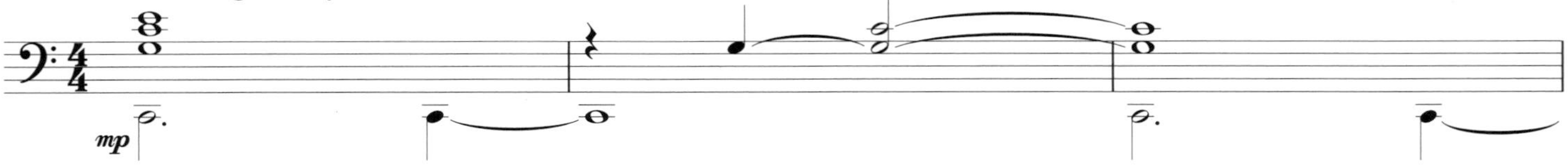

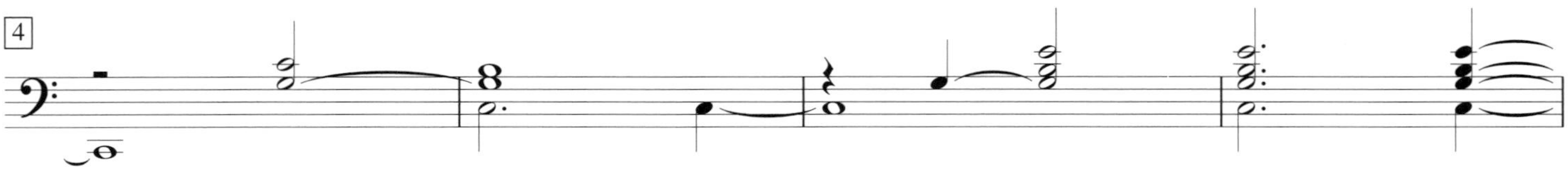

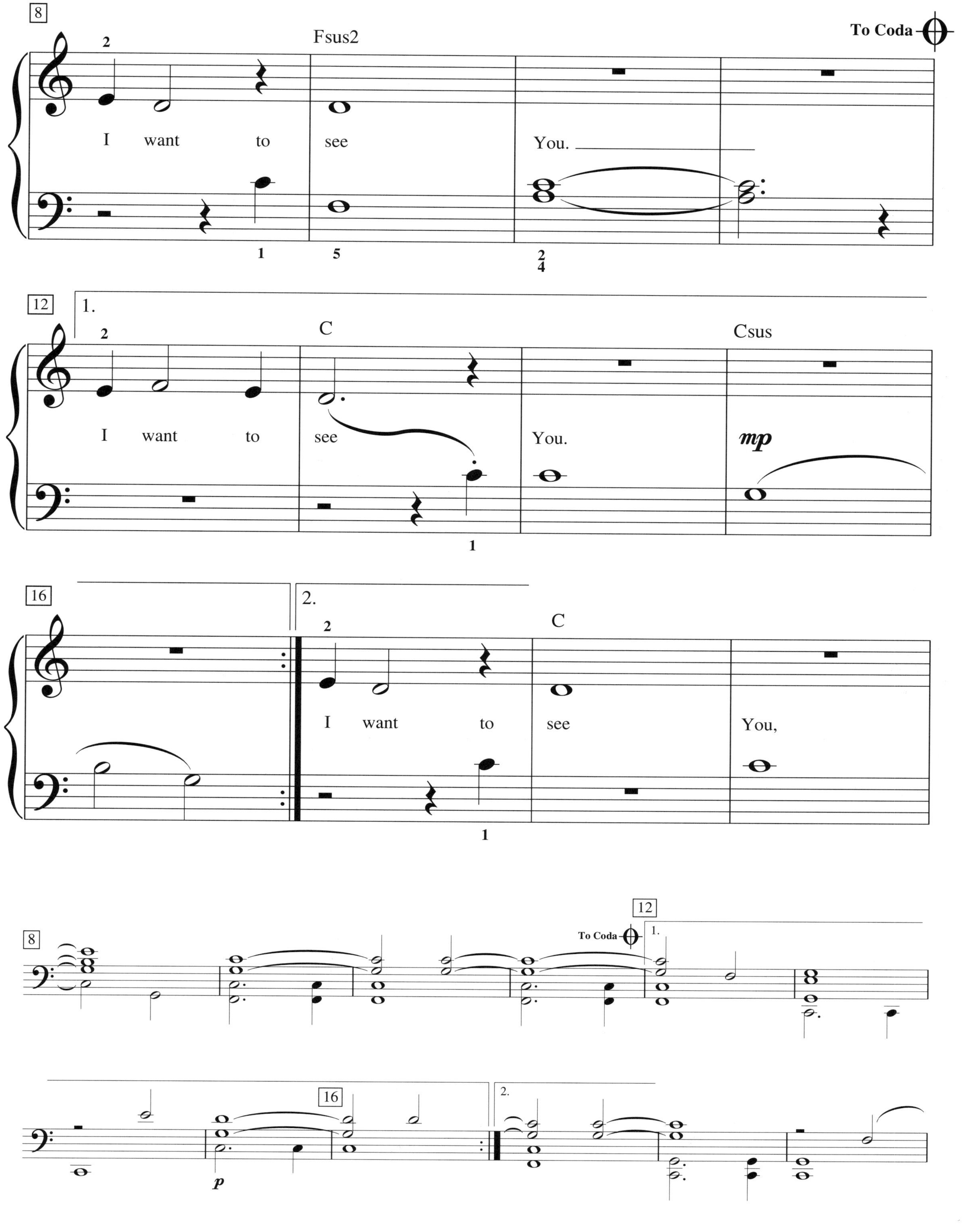
8
To Coda
Fsus2
I want to see You.
12
1.
C
Csus
I want to see You.
mp
16
2.
C
I want to see You,
8
To Coda
12
1.
16
2.
p

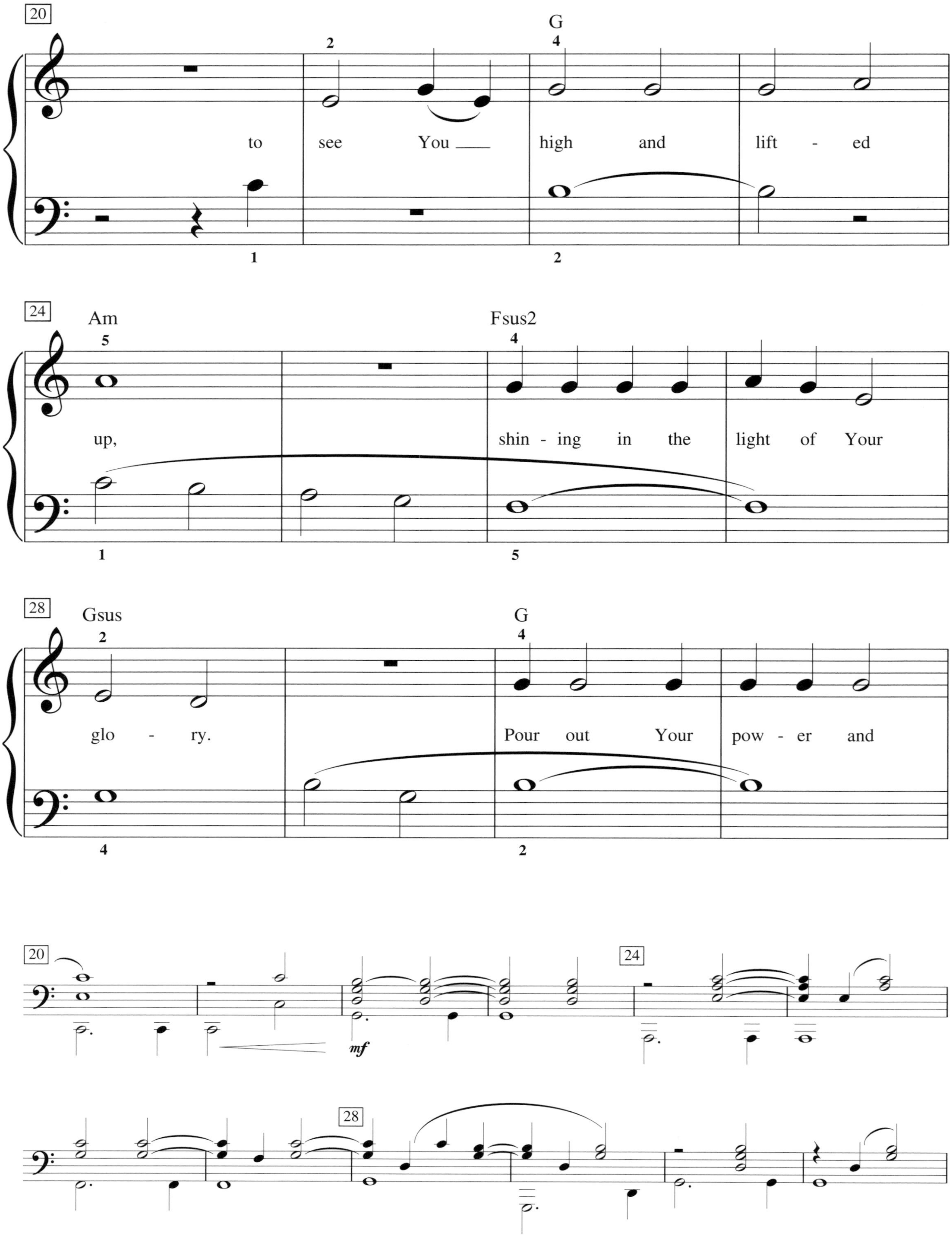
20
G
to see You high and lift - ed
24
Am
Fsus2
up, shin - ing in the light of Your
28
Gsus
G
glo - ry. Pour out Your pow - er and
20
mf
24
28

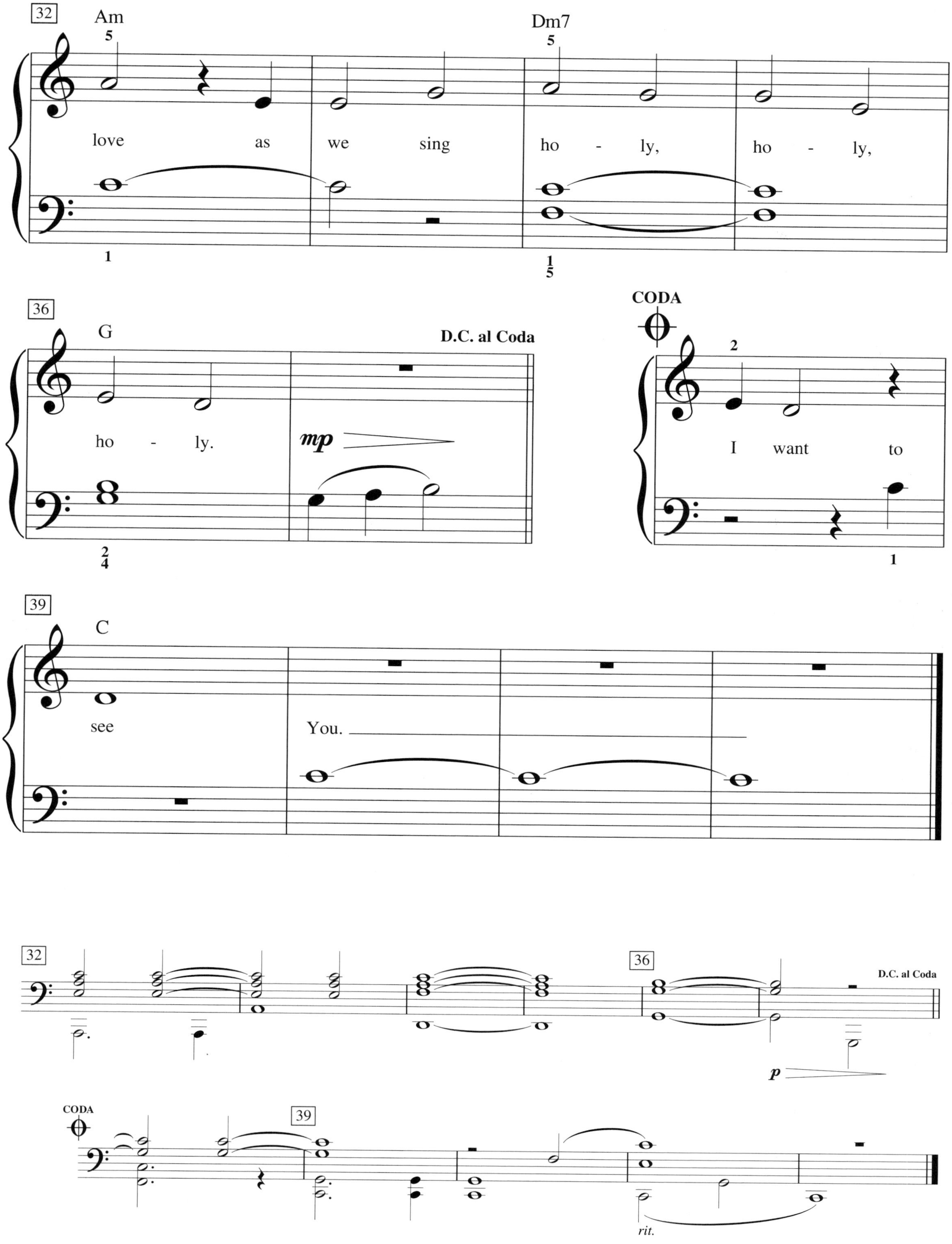
32
Am
Dm7
love as we sing ho - ly, ho - ly,
36
G
D.C. al Coda
ho - ly.
mp
CODA
I want to
39
C
see You.
32
36
D.C. al Coda
p
CODA
39
rit.

You Are So Good To Me

Words and Music by Don Chaffer,
Ben Pasley and Robin Pasley
Arranged by Deborah Brady

Moderate Rock, in "two" (𝅗𝅥 = 80)

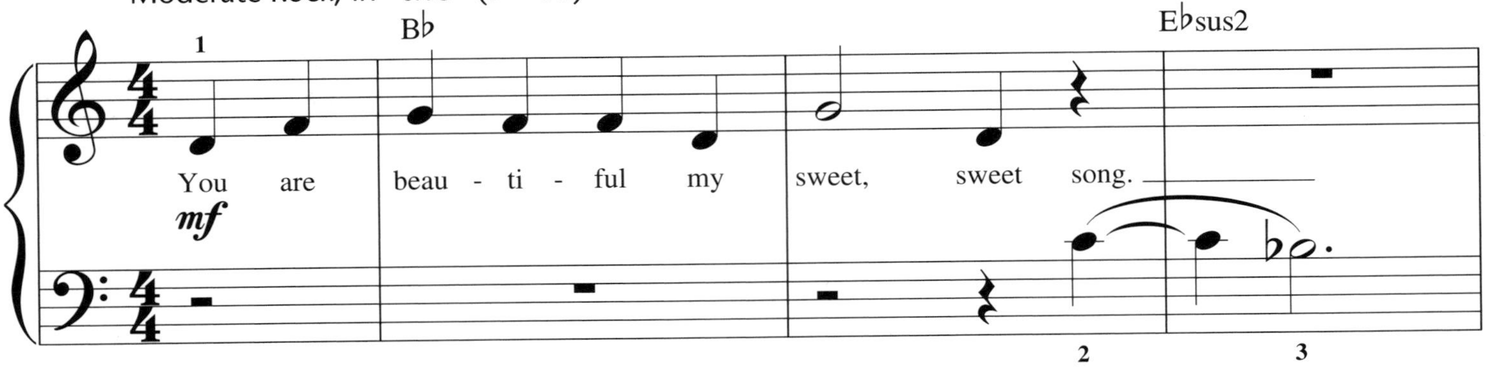

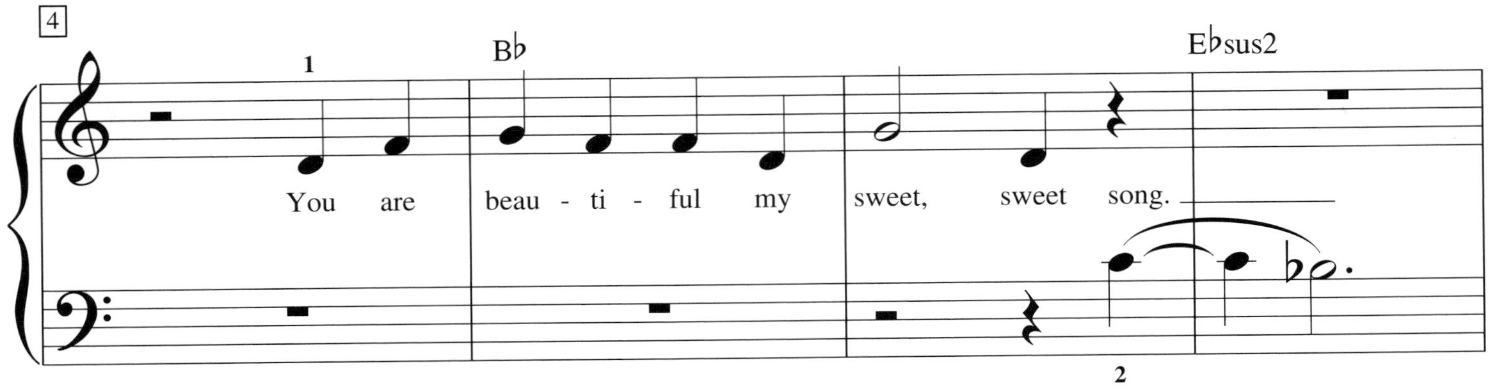

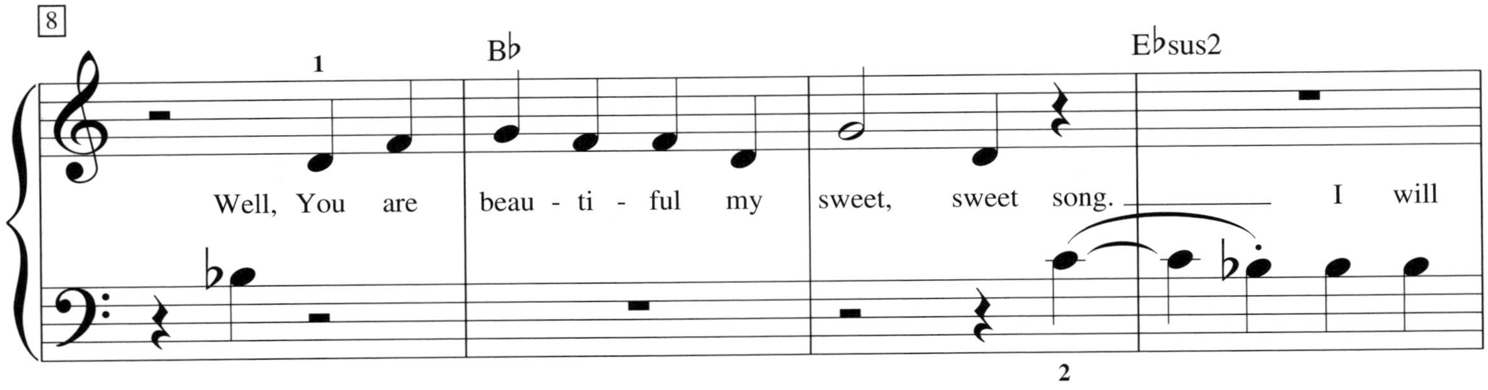

Accompaniment (Student plays one octave higher than written.)

Moderate Rock, in "two" (𝅗𝅥 = 80)

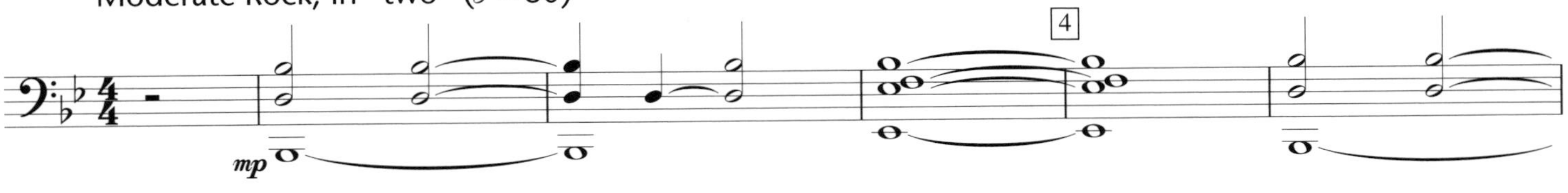

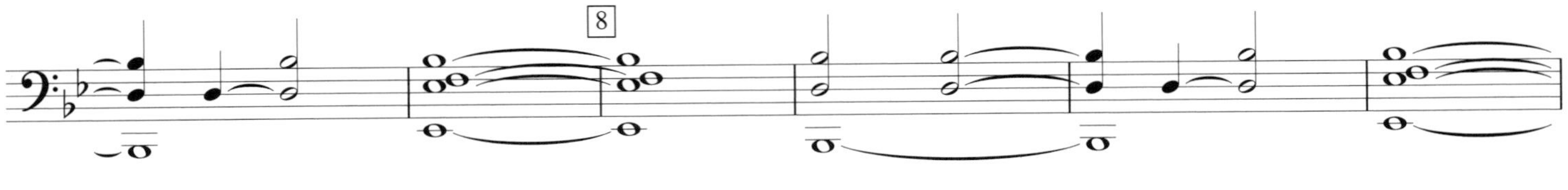

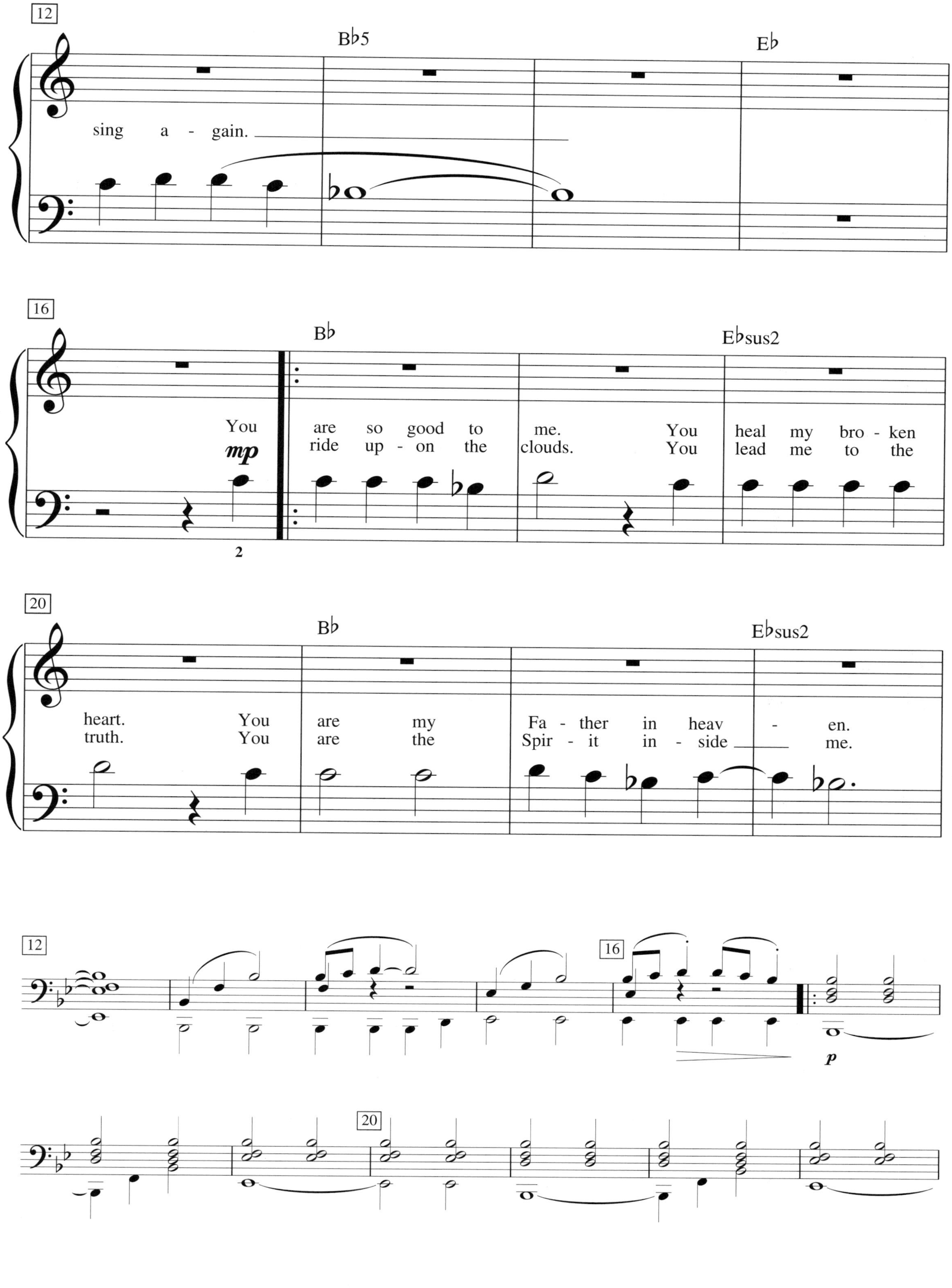
12
B♭5
E♭
sing a - gain.
16
B♭
E♭sus2
You are so good to me. You heal my bro - ken
ride up - on the clouds. You lead me to the
mp
2
20
B♭
E♭sus2
heart. You are my Fa - ther in heav - en.
truth. You are the Spir - it in - side me.
12
16
p
20

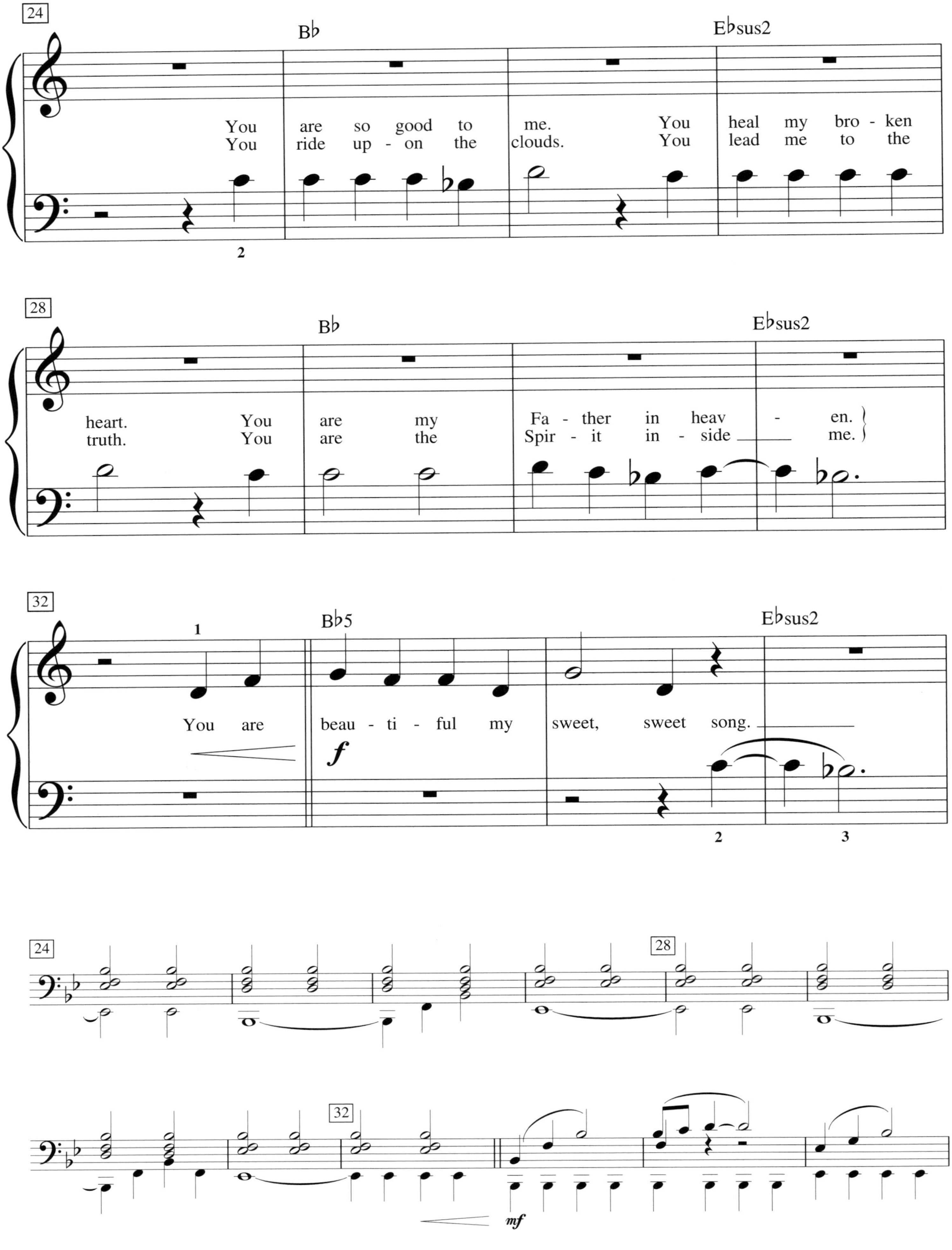
24
B♭
E♭sus2
You are so good to me. You heal my bro - ken
You ride up - on the clouds. You lead me to the
28
B♭
E♭sus2
heart. You are my Fa - ther in heav - en.
truth. You are the Spir - it in - side me.
32
B♭5
E♭sus2
You are beau - ti - ful my sweet, sweet song.
f
24
28
32
mf

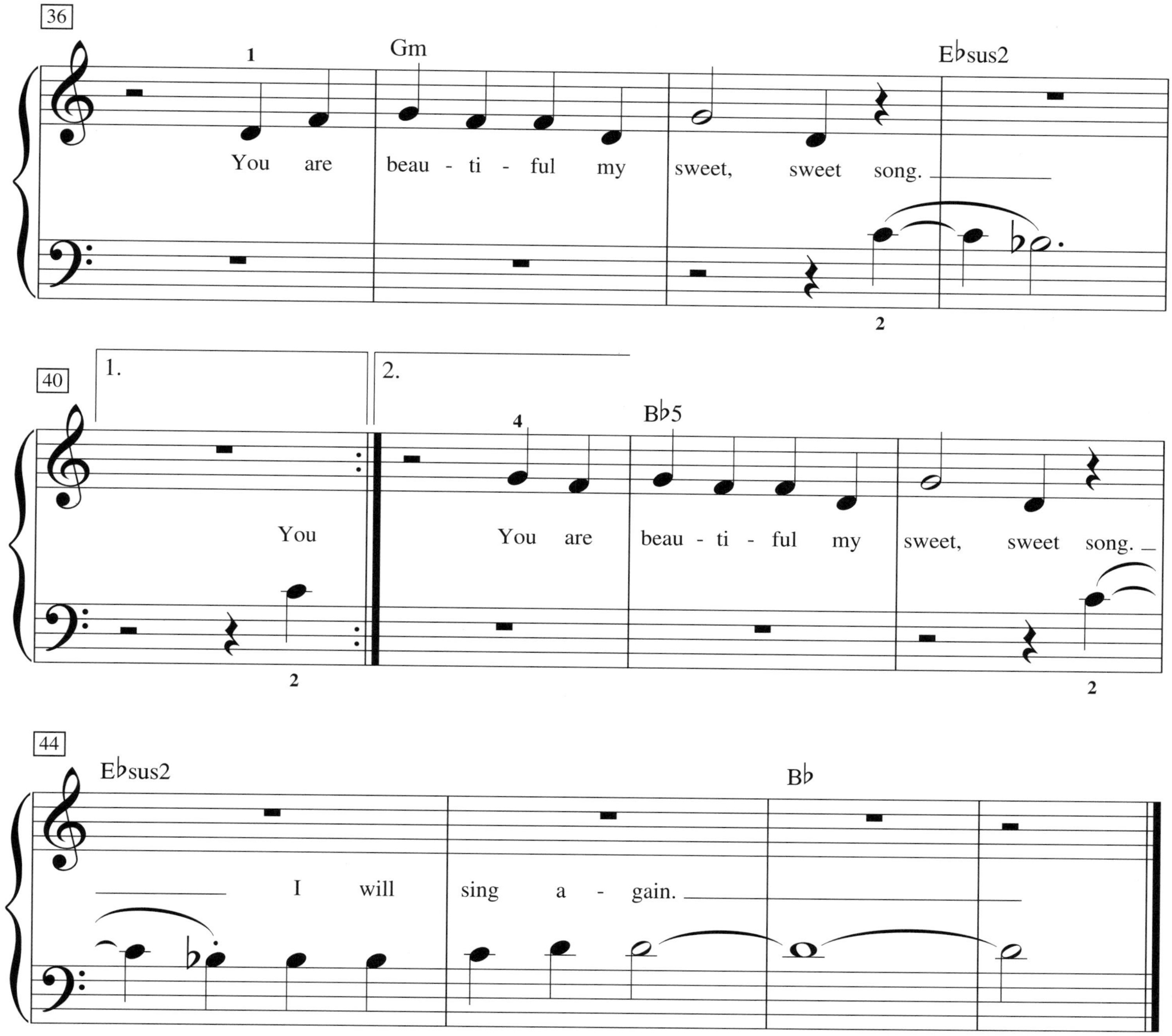
36
Gm
Ebsus2
You are beau - ti - ful my sweet, sweet song.
40
1.
2.
Bb5
You
You are beau - ti - ful my sweet, sweet song.
44
Ebsus2
Bb
I will sing a - gain.

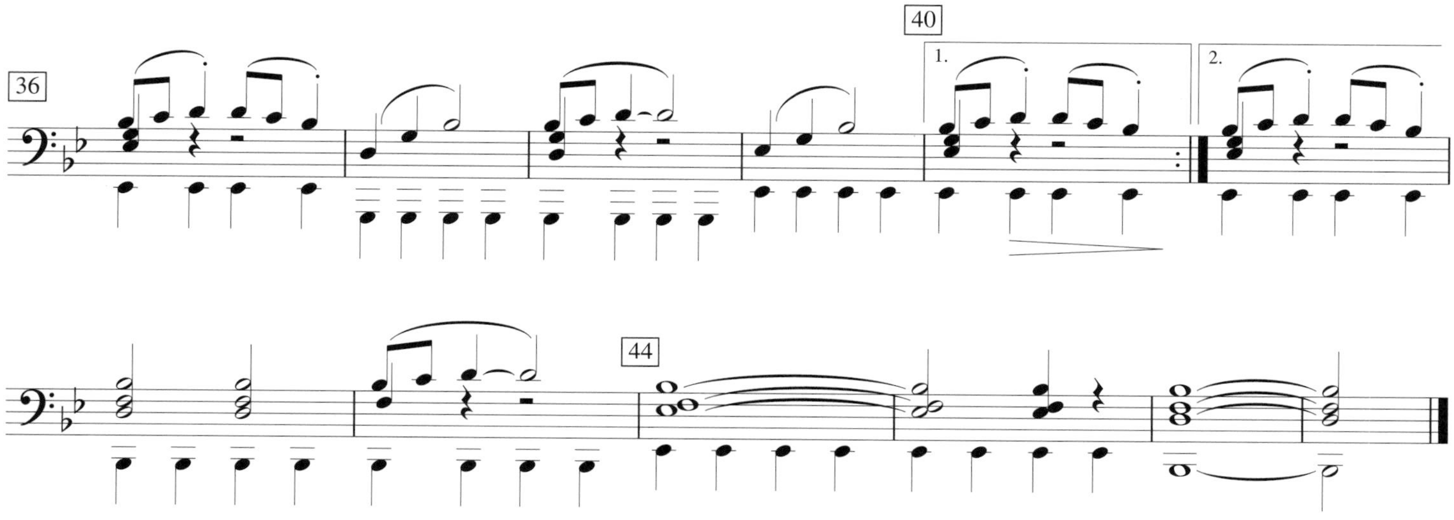
36
40
1.
2.
44

You Raise Me Up

Words and Music by Brendan Graham
and Rolf Lovland
Arranged by Deborah Brady

Freely, with much expression (♩ = 96)

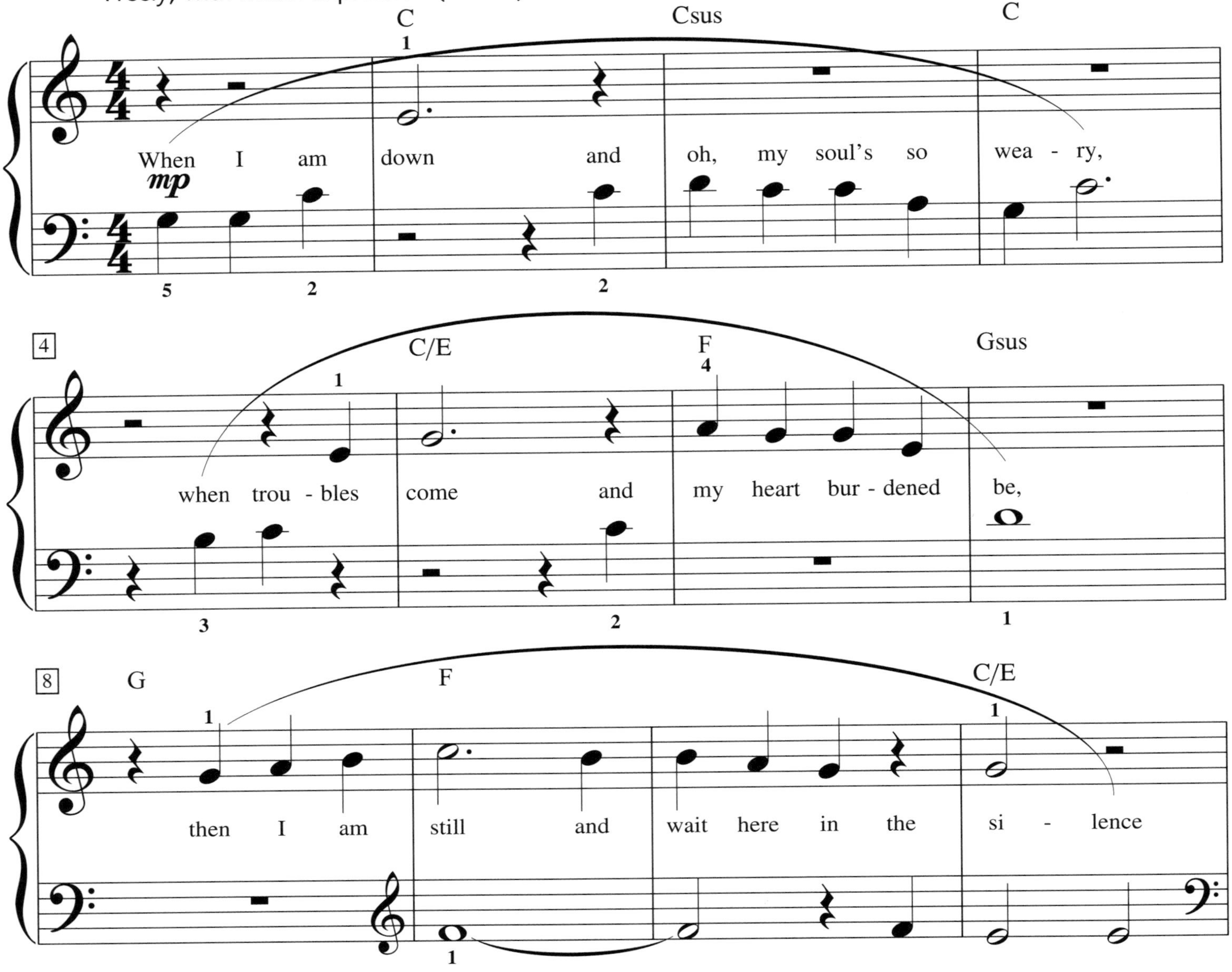

Accompaniment (Student plays one octave higher than written.)

Freely, with much expression (♩ = 96)

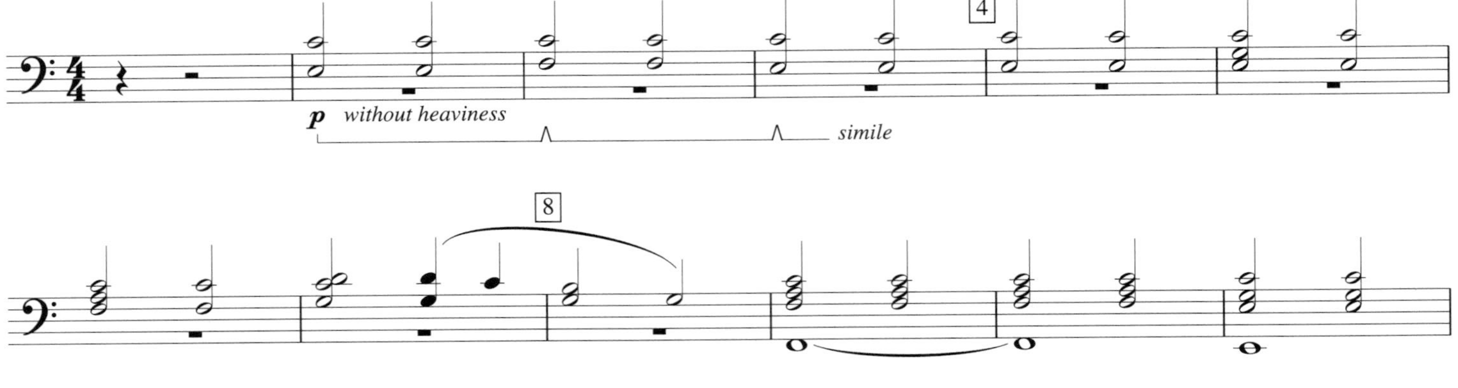

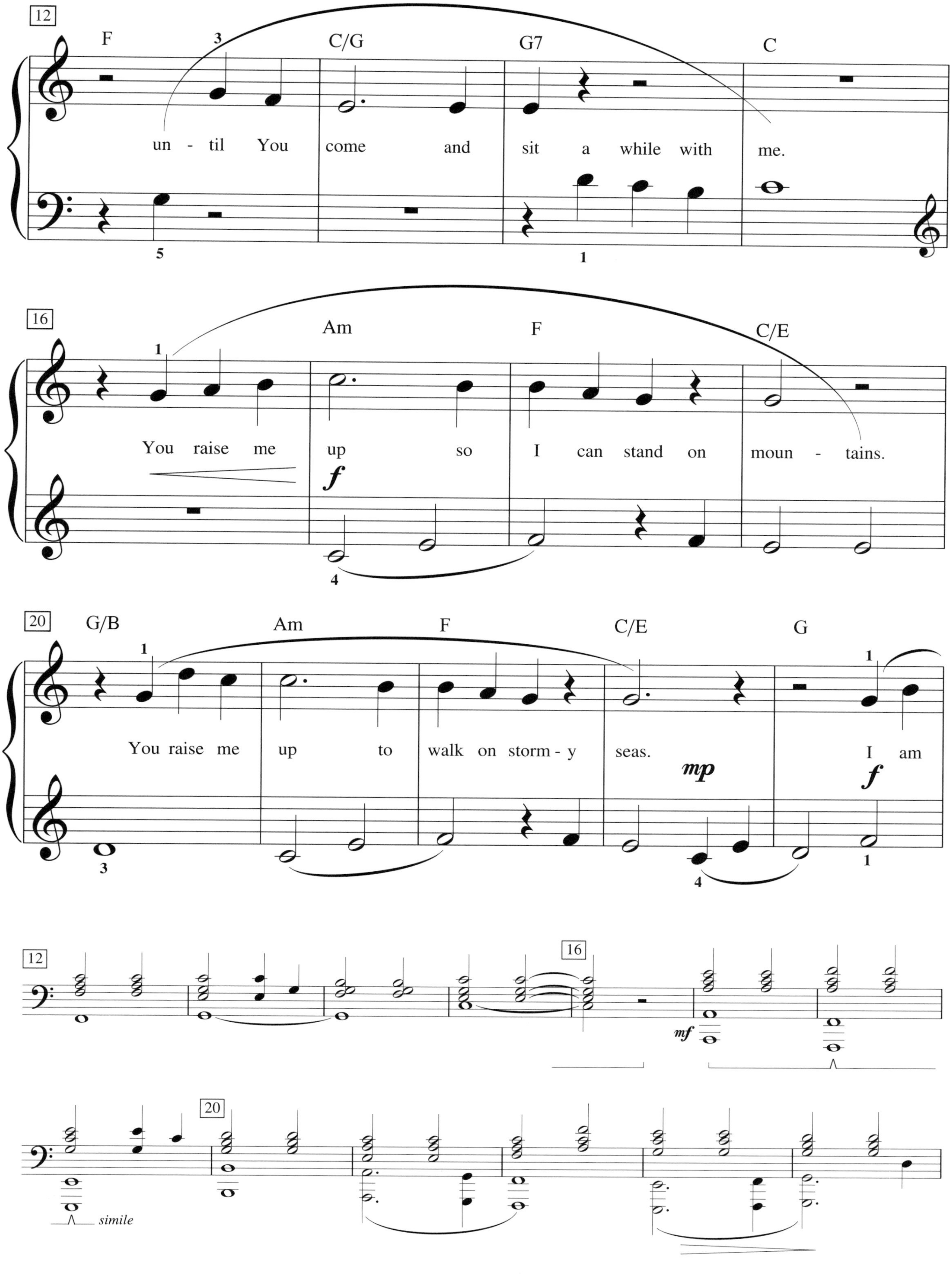
12
F C/G G7 C
un - til You come and sit a while with me.
16
Am F C/E
You raise me up so I can stand on moun - tains.
20
G/B Am F C/E G
You raise me up to walk on storm - y seas. I am
12
16
20
simile

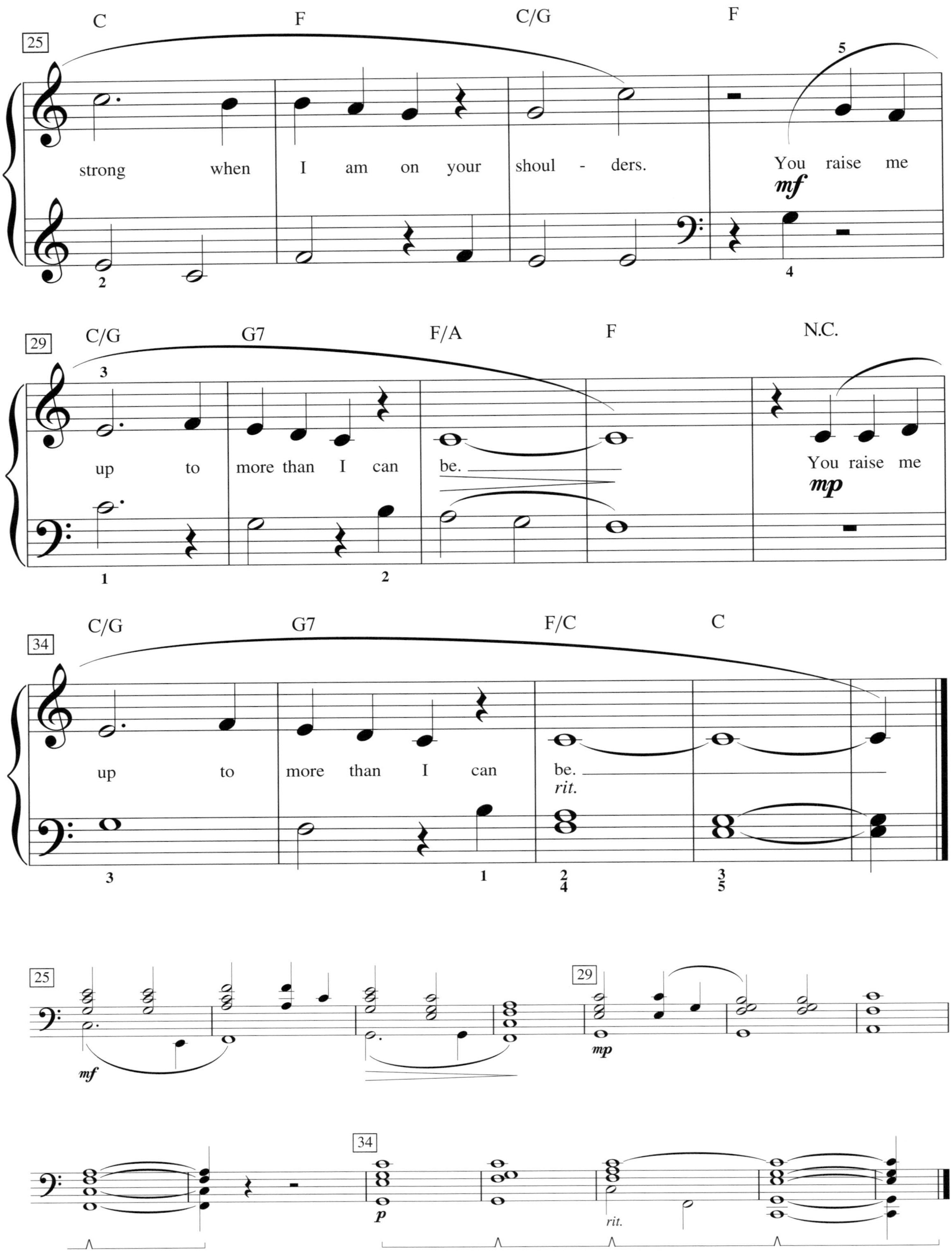
25
C F C/G F
strong when I am on your shoul - ders. You raise me
mf
29
C/G G7 F/A F N.C.
up to more than I can be. You raise me
mp
34
C/G G7 F/C C
up to more than I can be.
rit.
25
mf
29
mp
34
p
rit.

We Bow Down

Words and Music by Twila Paris
Arranged by Deborah Brady

Moderately, in "one" (♩. = 52)

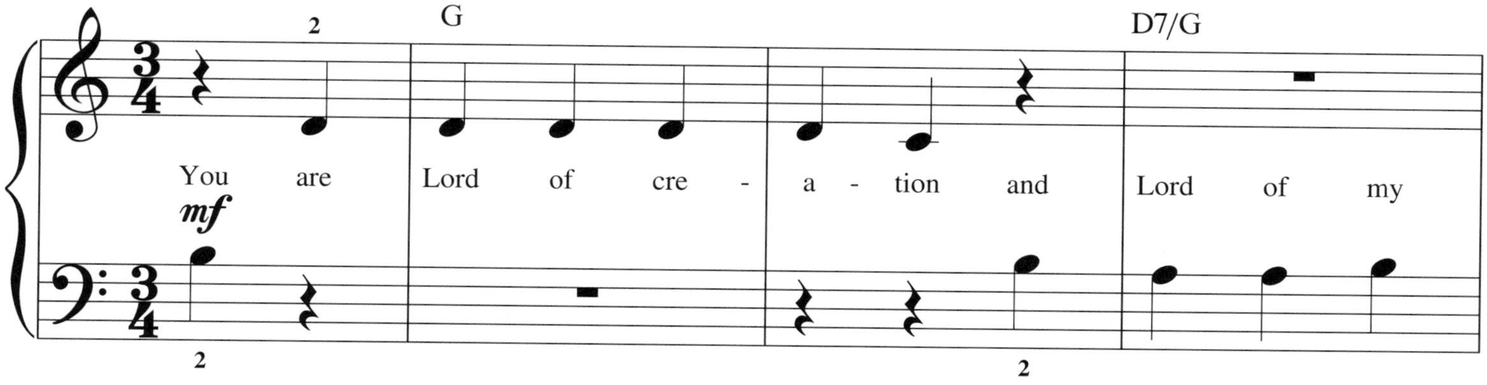

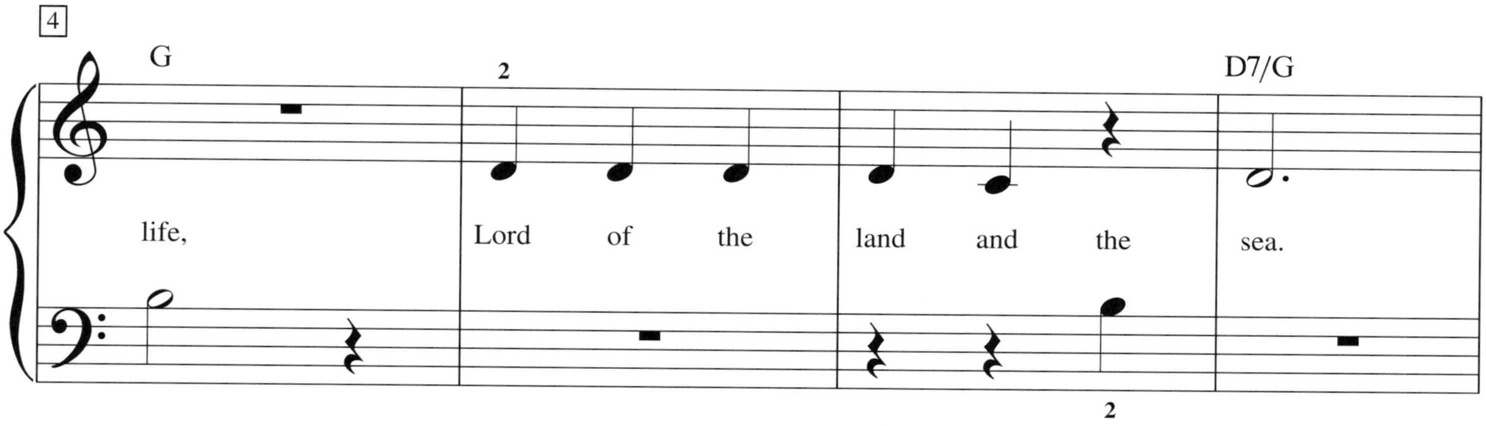

Accompaniment (Student plays two octaves higher than written.)

Moderately, in "one" (♩. = 52)

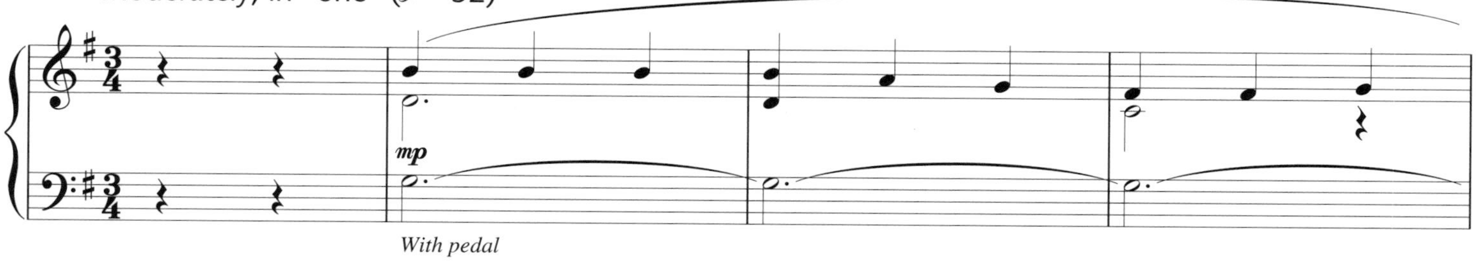

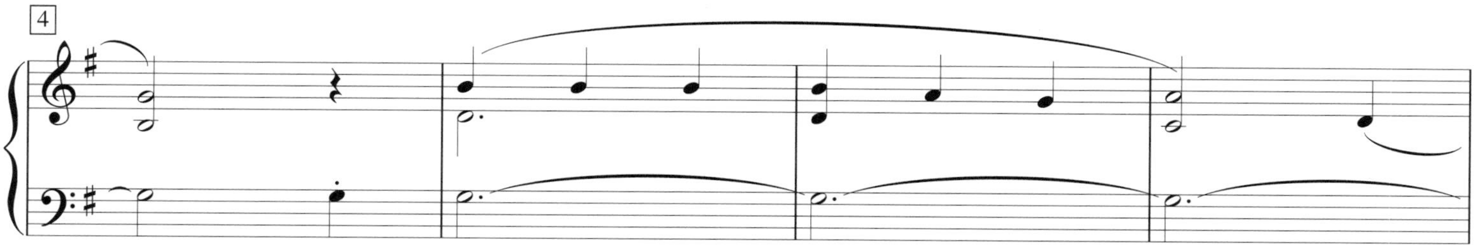

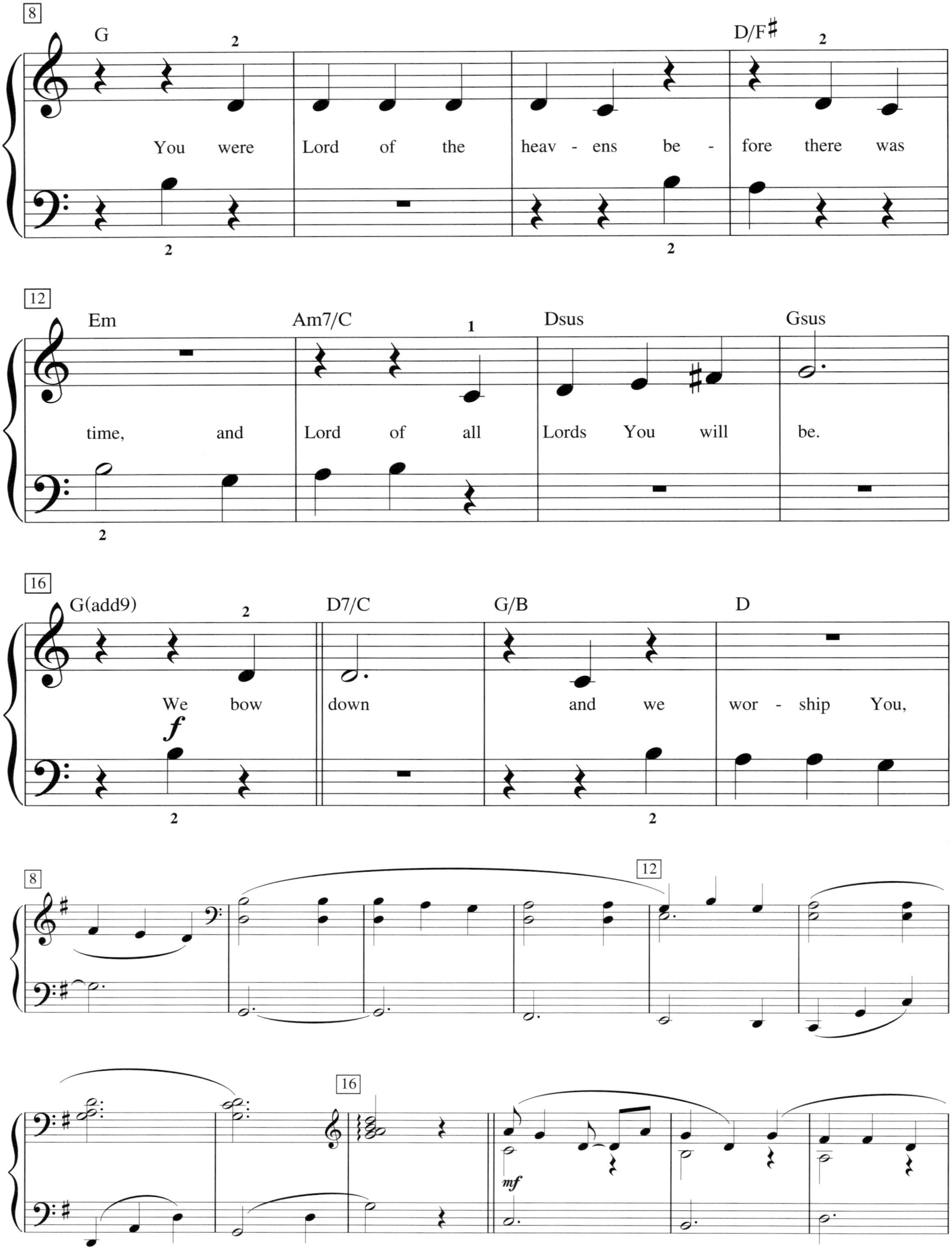
8
G
D/F♯
You were Lord of the heav - ens be - fore there was
12
Em
Am7/C
Dsus
Gsus
time, and Lord of all Lords You will be.
16
G(add9)
D7/C
G/B
D
We bow down and we wor - ship You,
f
8
12
16
mf

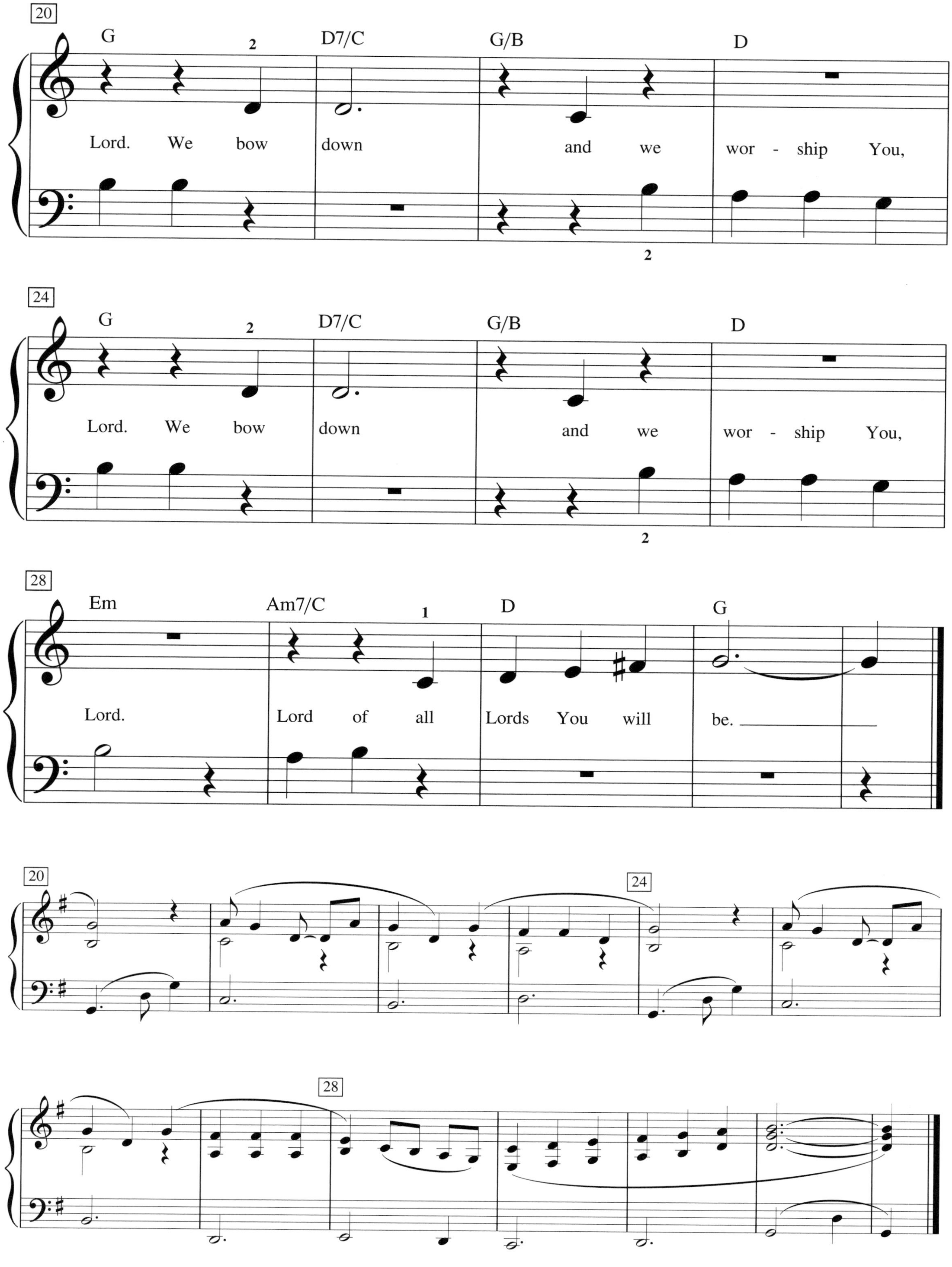
20
G
D7/C
G/B
D
Lord. We bow down and we wor - ship You,
24
G
D7/C
G/B
D
Lord. We bow down and we wor - ship You,
28
Em
Am7/C
D
G
Lord. Lord of all Lords You will be.
20
24
28

COMPOSER SHOWCASE
HAL LEONARD STUDENT PIANO LIBRARY

This series showcases the varied talents of our **Hal Leonard Student Piano Library** family of composers.

Here is where you will find great original piano music by your favorite composers, including Phillip Keveren, Carol Klose, Jennifer Linn, Bill Boyd, Bruce Berr, and many others. Carefully graded for easy selection, each book contains gems that are certain to become tomorrow's classics!

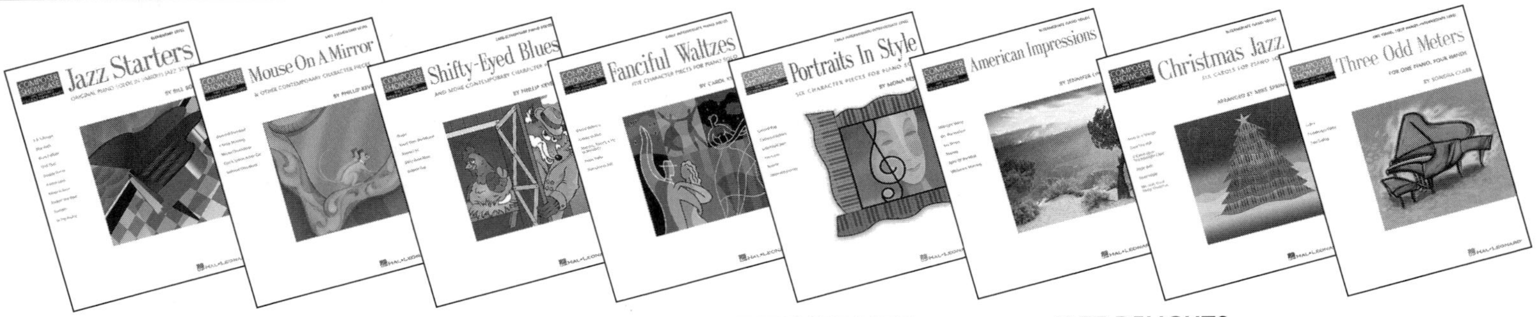

EARLY ELEMENTARY

JAZZ PRELIMS
by Bill Boyd
HL00290032 12 Solos........................$5.95

ELEMENTARY

JAZZ STARTERS I
by Bill Boyd
HL00290425 10 Solos........................$6.95

LATE ELEMENTARY

CORAL REEF SUITE
by Carol Klose
HL00296354 7 Solos........................$5.95

IMAGINATIONS IN STYLE
by Bruce Berr
HL00290359 7 Solos........................$5.95

JAZZ STARTERS II
by Bill Boyd
HL00290434 11 Solos........................$6.95

JAZZ STARTERS III
by Bill Boyd
HL00290465 12 Solos........................$6.95

MOUSE ON A MIRROR & OTHER CONTEMPORARY CHARACTER PIECES
by Phillip Keveren
HL00296361 5 Solos........................$6.95

PLAY THE BLUES!
by Luann Carman (Method Book)
HL00296357 10 Solos........................$7.95

SHIFTY-EYED BLUES – MORE CONTEMPORARY CHARACTER PIECES
by Phillip Keveren
HL00296374 5 Solos........................$6.95

TEX-MEX REX
by Phillip Keveren
HL00296353 6 Solos........................$5.95

THE TOYMAKER'S WORKSHOP
by Deborah Brady (1 Piano, 4 Hands)
HL00296513 5 Duets........................$5.95

TRADITIONAL CAROLS FOR TWO
arr. Carol Klose (1 Piano, 4 Hands)
HL00296557 5 Duets........................$6.95

For a full description and songlist for each of the books listed here, and to view the newest titles in this series, visit our website at **www.halleonard.com**

EARLY INTERMEDIATE

CHRISTMAS FOR TWO
arr. Dan Fox (1 Piano, 4 Hands)
HL00290069 4 Medley Duets $6.95

EXPEDITIONS IN STYLE
by Bruce Berr
HL00296526 11 Solos........................$6.95

EXPLORATIONS IN STYLE
by Bruce Berr
HL00290360 9 Solos........................$6.95

FANCIFUL WALTZES
by Carol Klose
HL00296473 5 Solos $7.95

JAZZ BITS (AND PIECES)
by Bill Boyd
HL00290312 11 Solos........................$6.95

MONDAY'S CHILD
by Deborah Brady
HL00296373 7 Solos........................$6.95

PORTRAITS IN STYLE
by Mona Rejino
HL00296507 6 Solos........................$6.95

THINK JAZZ!
by Bill Boyd (Method Book)
HL00290417..$9.95

WORLD GEMS
arr. Amy O'Grady (Piano Ens./2 Pianos, 8 Hands)
HL00296505 6 Folk Songs $6.95

INTERMEDIATE

AMERICAN IMPRESSIONS
by Jennifer Linn
HL00296471 6 Solos $7.95

ANIMAL TONE POEMS
by Michele Evans
HL00296439 10 Solos $6.95

CHRISTMAS JAZZ
arr. Mike Springer
HL00296525 6 Solos........................$6.95

CONCERTO FOR YOUNG PIANISTS
by Matthew Edwards (2 Pianos, 4 Hands)
HL00296356 Book/CD......................$16.95

DAKOTA DAYS
by Sondra Clark
HL00296521 5 Solos........................$6.95

FAVORITE CAROLS FOR TWO
arr. Sondra Clark (1 Piano, 4 Hands)
HL00296530 6 Duets........................$6.95

JAZZ DELIGHTS
by Bill Boyd
HL00240435 11 Solos........................$6.95

JAZZ FEST
by Bill Boyd
HL00240436 10 Solos........................$6.95

JAZZ SKETCHES
by Bill Boyd
HL00220001 8 Solos........................$6.95

JEROME KERN CLASSICS
arr. Eugénie Rocherolle
HL00296577 10 Solos.....................$12.95

LES PETITES IMPRESSIONS
by Jennifer Linn
HL00296355 6 Solos........................$6.95

MELODY TIMES TWO
arr. Eugénie Rocherolle (2 Pianos, 4 Hands)
HL00296360 4 Duos (2 Scores).......$12.95

POETIC MOMENTS
by Christos Tsitsaros
HL00296403 8 Solos........................$7.95

ROMP!
by Phillip Keveren
(Digital Ensemble/6 Keyboards, 6 Players)
HL00296549 Book/CD......................$9.95
HL00296548 Book/GM Disk $9.95

SONGS WITHOUT WORDS
by Christos Tsitsaros
HL00296506 9 Solos........................$7.95

SOUNDS OF CHRISTMAS
arr. Rosemary Barrett Byers (1 Piano, 4 Hands)
HL00296406 5 Duets........................$6.95

SOUNDS OF CHRISTMAS, VOL. 2
arr. Rosemary Barrett Byers (1 Piano, 4 Hands)
HL00296529 5 Duets........................$6.95

THREE ODD METERS
by Sondra Clark (1 Piano, 4 Hands)
HL00296472 3 Duets $6.95

THE TWELVE DAYS OF CHRISTMAS
by Deborah Brady
HL00296531 13 Solos $6.95

For More Information, See Your Local Music Dealer,
Or Write To:

HAL•LEONARD® CORPORATION
7777 W. Bluemound Rd. P.O. Box 13819 Milwaukee, WI 53213

Prices, contents & availability subject to change without notice.

0705